Healing
IN A
BROKEN
TUNNEL

Reflections on Navigating Trauma

ANGELA GOODEN

For information contact:

Angela Gooden, authorangelagooden@gmail.com

Developmental Writing Editor & Self-Publishing Consultant:

Sinyon Ducksworth, sinyon@letthepaperspeak.com

ISBN: 9798878584449
First Edition: February 2024

Contents

Where Do We Begin...   1

1. The Good Times   3

2. We Had Some Hills to Climb   6

3. When My Troubles Began   13

4. I Have Loved, and I Have Lost   19

5. The Road to Healing   25

6. Joy Comes in the Morning   33

Words of Encouragement   39

Contact the Author   41

Where Do We Begin...

This is not a success story. Not in the sense society counts success. I haven't slayed the dragon. I've only won some battles. I'm not living happily ever after in a house on a sunny hill surrounded by the scent of flowers in the air and the love of my life by my side.

There is a stench in the air. The pungency of war and its deadly aftermath. I just survived a bloody battle. And I'm tucked away, hiding out in the Lord. I'm surviving.

Someday, I hope I can write the story of a woman who is thriving and not just surviving. But this is all I have and yet I know it's so important to give. I am healing in this broken tunnel.

As I sit and steal this moment of peace, reflecting on how thankful I am to still be here through it all, letting my wounds heal, as war rages on somewhere, I want to write to you, dear friend. You are somewhere further down in the valley, catching one loss after another, holding on to the hope that there is a light ahead.

These reflections of my journey through trauma are my little flickering lights of hope to you. To let you know that I'm just like you. I've come up in some trying and hard circumstances like you. I've made some mistakes. I've walked with God and away from him. Then back again. I've traversed through some muddy waters. I've fought some ugly battles. I've lost and somehow managed to get myself up, dust off and stand.

All I can do these days is stand. Sometimes, wobbly, sometimes hunched over, and sometimes crawling on my hands and knees, realizing that this is a form of *standing* too. What brings me hope is knowing I am not alone. There is a God. The very fact that these pages breathe victory despite it all is a testimony to God's power in my life. And his keeping power is in your life too.

I continue to pray for you, friend. Continue to pray for me too. I need it. There is yet still a journey ahead of me.

But in the words of the Apostle Paul:

I'm not saying that I have this all together, that I have it made. But I am well on my way, reaching out for Christ, who has so wondrously reached out for me. Friends, don't get me wrong: By no means do I count myself an expert in all of this, but I've got my eye on the goal, where God is beckoning us onward—to Jesus. I'm off and running, and I'm not turning back (Philippians 3:12-14, MSG).

Neither height nor depth, nor anything else in all creation, will be able to separate us from the love of God that is in Christ Jesus our Lord (Romans 8:39, NIV).

CHAPTER 1

The Good Times

I WAS RAISED IN a family of five brothers and one sister. I grew up in a country community outside of Mount Olive, Mississippi, walking distance from Lilly Valley Missionary Baptist Church. Like other kids in my community, that church was part of our upbringing, a cornerstone of our rural neighborhood. It kept us busy and engaged in fun activities.

My Mother, Annie Ducksworth, and my Father, Emerson Edison knew the importance of giving their kids a foundation in the Lord, like all southern parents who still kept to the old traditional ways of living. And like many, if they were not consistent themselves, we kids still had to go.

I was a choir singer and a drill team member. As a choir singer, I visited church revivals, sang during pastor appreciation days, and other occasions I fondly remember. In the drill team, we performed and competed against other drill teams. We won trophies and quoted bible verses.

In school science and math were my favorite subjects. I enjoyed doing science projects. On holidays like Thanksgiving and Christmas, I remember my dad always coming to eat lunch with me, our little tradition. Truly a daddy's girl, I was ready for these occasions. Also because I knew I wasn't gonna drink the cafeteria milk because he got me soda. My dad always came to school to check on me. Before he left he always made sure to give me snack money.

In elementary, I remember winning Ms. Hopewell in sixth grade, our little equivalent to homecoming queen. I remember Mom taking me to get my hair done and looking for dresses. I was so happy.

My mom and dad are heroes to me. Their love was true and known. My siblings and I always had what we needed. If we didn't have it, my parents were going to make a way to get it. I am grateful and blessed to have them as my parents. On Mother's Day and Father's Day, my siblings and I made sure they knew how much they were appreciated.

In truth, all of us have been trouble for them in some type of way. But they taught us the right way to the best of their ability and remained loving us regardless of what we did.

I wanted to start this journey by acknowledging the good I had in my life growing up and the foundations that were laid for me. However, this still did not stop trauma from entering my world.

Reflection 1 - Your Beginnings

Before you journey on, take time to reflect on the good you remember about your beginnings and the positive things about your childhood that have shaped you today.

CHAPTER 2

We Had Some Hills to Climb

IT STILL BAFFLES ME how my mother struggled through so much but still made it happen for my siblings and me. If she didn't have it she was going to get it. Mom was encouraging and always wanted the best for us all. Family unity has always been a big deal to her. She will do whatever it takes to keep us together. She always told us to love one another and show respect. Even though sometimes we didn't listen, her words always remain in our hearts.

My mom had me and two of my brothers by my dad. And I've already told you how much I was a daddy's girl, may he rest in peace. My Dad was smart, stern, and loved dressing up in his suits, khaki pants, and button-down shirts with his Stacey Adams shoes. He would give us the world but one thing for sure, you were going to obey him. He didn't play.

I remember at the age of fifteen when I first got my driver's license in Jackson, MS. My godfather, Johnny Fairley, took me there. My mother had fussed the night before because I hadn't studied the book for the written portion of the test. I hopped my behind in the car anyway when Johnny pulled up. As we headed to Jackson, I opened up the book. By the time we arrived an hour or so later, I had given myself a crash course on everything I felt I needed to know. All else would be left up to chance, but I was determined. And sure enough, I breezed right through that written test. Then it was time for the actual driving test. My godfather like always was standing there rooting for me. I received my license that day.

I arrived back home and jumped out of the car headed straight to my mother, vindicated and flashing my license, exclaiming, "*Who said, who said, I wasn't gonna get my license?*"

I was so proud of myself. My mother was shocked but proud too!

Johnny Fairley was always an inspiration in my life. He always told me that I could do whatever I put my mind to. He was big on education as well. He is one of the reasons today why I give it my all in wherever life takes me.

But as I was saying before, my mother has been in many struggles. If she were writing her story, I don't think there would be enough pages or ink to hold the heartache, grief, and trauma my mother has endured over her lifetime. I used to watch her walk around the house singing her gospels and crying. Something about it, my young mind couldn't understand rubbed my heart the wrong way.

But she would say, "These are tears of joy." I get it now.

My mom lost her dad, then her mother, and soon after that her son. The overwhelming grief of it all caused her to have a nervous breakdown. She eventually got back to normal but it was some hard scary times in the valley, in the storms, in the tunnel. I thank God he brought her back out. I think of her as my sunshine. The rain, wind, and fire came but the sun still shines somehow.

My big brother, Kevin whom most knew as Goobie, died from leukemia on August 21, 1997. Because we shared the same birthday, we used to celebrate together. I remember when the bus pulled up he would be standing beside the road waiting for me just to say Happy Birthday. It was the little things from him that made me smile. Short but tough, he was a force in the earth.

My oldest brother, Curtis had hemophilia and so does my baby brother, Emerson Jr. It was a trait that ran in our family through the women, they said. If we got pregnant with a boy it was a good chance that they could have the blood disorder. My mom used to stay away from the house for days to weeks and maybe months with them. Jackson University Hospital became her second home. If it wasn't Curtis sick, it was Emerson. I know her body was tired and weary but she kept going. I couldn't ask God for a better mother, father, or family. Annie Owens will always be the world's greatest mom for all she has given, and taken, yet still kept going for us.

My brother Curtis was smart and had one of the best handwriting styles you could ever see. I remember when he used to make us purses out of potato chip bags! He was good at tinting windows and loved riding on motorcycles. An all-around creative soul, he was also good at drawing and cutting hair. In our community, he made some of the best CD mixes and DVDs. Curtis was friendly and had a big smile that would brighten your day.

My brother Emerson is a prayer warrior. He can say a prayer that would touch you so deeply and make you cry. He has been sickly all his life but thanks to God, still standing. Emerson is also short like Goobie was but tough too. My brother, James is a good dancer. He loves to dance. It's like he hears music and his feet can't help but get happy. Before you know it, he's on the floor. Those moments make us as a family smile, throw off our burdens, and enjoy each other. I remember one year at our family reunion they had a dancing contest. Guess who got out there and won, James did! He is sweet at heart, caring, and so funny.

My sister and I used to dress alike and occasionally went out together. She is fun to be around and very funny as well. We argue at times and disagree on things but our love remains true, like Mama would want. Mom named her Annie Merle but she didn't like that name. Everyone calls her Honey. I used to ask her how she got that name.

"Cause I'm sweet like honey," she would tease.

My sister has been through her own life battles and maybe still battling some things. But she knows Jesus. And most importantly, He still has her in his hands. My sister loves her wigs and makeup. She will spend hours in the mirror making sure that hair is on point. She is the type that lets things roll off her back, she refuses to be weary, she'd tell you. She is a strong woman. And if you walked a mile in her shoes, you'd know that you would have to be if you were still standing.

My brother Curtis married Patricia Keyes Owens. I couldn't ask for a better sis-n-law. She is sweet, humble, loving, caring, and loves going to church. She stood by my brother's side and took great care of him until he passed away on May 25, 2015. Today, she still comes around and shows the same love to our family. My brother and Patricia gave us our beloved niece, Deja Owens, and nephew, Curvin Owens.

Back on December 25, 1991, we lost James Allen. My three brothers and I had all gotten bikes for Christmas. We were so excited and happy about going riding on them that morning. As we chilled at the end of Mom's driveway we discussed which way we would bike, take the more hilly route of the residential country road which would prove a more challenging ride. Or bike right, up towards the church. Emerson and James were parked on their bikes more off the road on my left side and James Allen was on my right, closer to the street.

I remember seeing a car flying over the hill and stumbling off the road as it came near us. It happened so fast, with no time to even think, yet everything seemed in slow motion at the same time. And then the car veered off to the side of the street again, right before my eyes. And I watched James Allen's little body float in the air and drop down on the paved road. Some drunk lady was driving. She knew she hit something but she kept going, dragging my brother's bike under her car as she plowed on up the road.

Emerson and James ran into the house. I was in shock and couldn't move. I just stared at where James Allen had landed. He was only five years old and I was seven. At some point, my body finally became unglued from my bike and was moving towards him. I tried my best to get to where he was but the closer I got something kept turning me around. As I reflect on it today, I know it was God's mercy on my little soul because no seven-year-old should see their brother's broken body lying in the street like that. God only allowed me to see so much. And every year, every Christmas, I replay that moment in my head. It's been years and I can still remember like it was yesterday. I carry this with me every day of my life and the anxiety that comes along with it.

When my brothers ran into the house that day, my mom ran out. She stumbled to the street where her son lay. I can still hear that agonizing wail that came from her. Her painful cries, her hands grabbing fists full of her hair. We cried too. There was no response from James Allen. The heart-wrenching anguish and intensity, as the tears flowed down my dad's face pushed me further in despair. He took all the bikes away that day. But it wasn't a loss to us. We didn't want to ride them anyway after what we had seen. We knew our brother was gone and we were terrified. We all slept together that night in the same bed holding on to each other for dear life.

I didn't get to know much of James Allen but I remember what he looked like. I remember the way he smiled. I remember every weekend I would go stay with our Aunt Maggie who is now deceased. She would take me to church every Sunday with her. She lived in Hebron, MS. One day James Allen insisted on going to Aunt Maggie's just because I was going. Before the day was over, Mom had to pick him up cause he cried to go back home. I chuckled. These are the things that I remember about my brother and I also carry with me every day of my life.

Long live all my brothers that have gone on home to glory. The memories I have of them, our love for each other, and the times that we have shared, I will never forget.

Reflection 2 - The Painful Memories

Are there some things from your childhood that you are still processing today? How are you coping? What I am learning is that it is never too late to seek support to help you through healing no matter how long ago a tragedy occurred in your life.

Listen to the song, "I Won't Complain" by Rev. Paul Jones. Then write down three things you are grateful for.

CHAPTER 3

When My Troubles Began

As a young teen, I attended school at Collins Middle School in Collins, Mississippi. I joined the basketball team and enjoyed playing. I had my first school fight in middle school as well and that seemed to become a new normal. I was the type that wanted to be the pretty girl. My parents allowed me to wear what I liked in my clothing and shoe choices. As a result, I attracted all types of attention. And with attention comes those who wait for opportunities to cut you down.

At times, I was bothered by classmates who loved to bully or dislike others for no reason. So I got fed up one day and spoke up. Classmates, waiting for a reason to have beef, turned on me. This is where the fighting began, but somewhere along the way, it seemed all I did was get caught up in one altercation after another with someone, for one reason or another until it all became so toxic, that it made me sick. Yet, I lost myself somewhere in all the drama and could not untangle all the webs to weave my way out.

By my Junior year of High School, I managed to cultivate a few close friends. We attended parties, hung out together, and had sleepovers. During those days, all the great parties went down at the local National Guard center. I loved to dance and one night, I caught the eye of a guy named, Cody. Every time after that night when I ran into him he would approach me. He was crushing on me hard, as we used to say. One day during school lunch my friends and I were deep in girl chat. We talked about parties we had attended, parties we were planning to attend, and boys. A girl named Janice brought up Cody. And just like any other girl, I made it known that he was digging me.

Janice was a classmate and friend. I used to go stay with her at times over the weekend. We would sit in her room and listen to music, sing, and talk on the phone. Well, I realized Janice liked Cody a lot. Although I wasn't into him, I did want her to know he was trying to holler. But she didn't see it that way. She got mad and turned her back on me.

Our friendship was officially over and a trail of damage would follow. I was also friends with Janice's cousin, Sherry. Sherry used to get dropped off at my house every morning by the bus driver as he made pickups around the Lily Valley community. My mom would have jeans and shirts laid out and Sherry would pick out what she wanted to wear. I always had the hair accessories laid out for her to fix her hair before the bus made its way back around to pick us up. Our bus driver was really cool like that, looking out for us when he could. I'm assuming that Janice told Sherry about the Cody situation and had Sherry stop being friends with me because she stopped getting off at my house. Up until that point, the Cody thing wasn't that big of a deal to me but I realized how deep it was for Janice. Janice and Sherry started treating me cold and other girls on the bus joined them.

My mother would get up early in the morning and cook breakfast for us before we got on the bus. She would bake biscuits, fry eggs, bacon and sausage. My brothers and I excitedly would eat up. But every morning those groups of girls would be waiting for me to get on the bus just to holler out "Eggs!" You could smell Mom's breakfast on us. But the girls took it as an opportunity to accuse me of smelling like rotten eggs, their morning laughs to set them about their day and make them feel big, attempting to make me feel as low as I guess Janice felt. All because a boy I had no control over, liked me and not her.

Who cares about the boy, I thought. It was devastating to lose what little friendships I had. That one statement, confessing that he liked me, created many enemies. It played over in my mind and I wondered if I should have kept it all to myself. So as they hit me with their ugly words *every* morning on the bus, I said nothing. I heard it but never spoke about it. Their taunting kept happening up until my fight with Sherry. Janice put her up to it. To coax the fight out of me. And I gave it to her.

Sherry had a box cutter that I didn't see until it would prove too late. The others knew. While we were duking it out, I could feel the other girls closing in on me and casting their licks. And then I was cut across the face. Our bus driver took us immediately to school administration, and we remained there until they suspended us and sent us home.

After the suspension was over, I couldn't return to school until I attended a meeting with the district's school board. When I attended the meeting, I found out that the group of girls had all lied and written statements against me saying that I brought the box cutter to school. My bus driver even wrote a statement against me. I was very disappointed in him because in my heart I felt that he was taking sides although he knew it was a lie. I would go on to hold a grudge with them all for that.

I wanted to prove to the school board that it was all a lie so I desperately pleaded with them to give me a lie detector test. I told them that my mom and dad would even pay for it to be administered. But Mama and Daddy couldn't rescue me from this one. Because of all those previous fights I'd had over the years, the board was not trying to hear anything I had to say. My tainted history had told them all they needed to know. I was so disappointed. This was my life, my education, and it was all taken from me within a blink of an eye.

After the meeting with them, we had to wait to hear the decision that was made. They wanted me to spend my senior year at the Alternative School. I couldn't attend basketball or football games. We had the VoTech, a vocational education center next to our high school, where I attended skill and trade classes. I could no longer attend Votech. I wasn't allowed to go to my senior prom. All my privileges were taken away.

I attended the Alternative school for about a month and got so discouraged. I remember going home crying to my mother and father, "I can't do this; I'm not supposed to be in there!"

My mom and dad hated that for me, but it was nothing that they could do. I attended alternative school for about another month and decided I had enough. My soul was hurt. I had lost all focus. I talked to one of my teachers about what I was feeling. He begged me not to drop out. He reminded me of how good my grades were and that it was my last year, I could make it if I just held on. But I just couldn't accept the fact of having to be there, so I eventually dropped out anyway.

It wasn't long after that Sherry came to me and apologized. I forgave her but I didn't forget. I never forgot. Years after, the 'Class of 2003', would send me invites about class reunions and gatherings, but I never attended. I didn't feel part of the class. I had been burned hard, anything affiliated with high school memories was stained. I was bitter and broken, and attending events with old classmates sharing senior year memories of prom and school events would only cut new slashes in my old wounds.

Reflection 3 - What were your significant moments?

Can you reflect on that moment or key moments in your life that changed things for you and left a lasting negative imprint? Sometimes to see how you start setting things right, you gotta recognize where things went wrong.

CHAPTER 4

I Have Loved, and I Have Lost

I BEGAN DATING IN middle school. I was in a relationship with my first love, Joseph. In high school, I got pregnant. I remember fainting in front of the locker that we shared. I wasn't eating much and while I could get by for myself, my body didn't have the energy to support both me and the baby girl growing inside of me. I remember Joseph scooping me up off the floor and taking me to the front office. I was sent home that day. And Joseph started picking me up for school after that, giving me more time and peace to eat breakfast each morning. I still rode the bus in the afternoons as Joseph was older than me and got out of school early.

I was sixteen and pregnant by my nineteen-year-old boyfriend. It hurt my mom, and I was disappointed in myself too that I'd gotten pregnant so young. But I had to keep going for my baby girl, Angelica Owens. I adored that little girl. She gave me a reason to smile in bad times.

Joseph's maturity began to rub off on me. He taught me my first cooking lessons. Encouraged me to take better care of myself. And I knew I needed to for our Angelica. I loved that Joseph was hardworking and dedicated. He was good for me and a great father to our baby girl. Still, it wasn't enough to hold me. While determined to be a good mom, I was still too young to be a dedicated girlfriend to Joseph. I didn't make all the best decisions in my relationship with him.

Problems started occurring, he wronged me, and I wronged him. In all of that, I had my second child. A baby boy, Joseph Owens. Yet, Joseph remained dedicated, still there providing for us. Somewhere down the line, my relationship with my school sweetheart inevitably ended. Today he remains dedicated, hard-working, and A Great Father.

After Joseph, I gradually moved on. Days turned into weeks, weeks turned into months and finally, I was ready to find someone to build a life with. That's when I met Eric Gooden.

Eric was my prince charming. We dated for about two years and I gave birth to my third child, Akeelah Gooden. During those days, I was happy and in love. Three years later, it was still Eric and Angela. And I got pregnant with our baby boy, my fourth child. Eric and I decided to get married while I was pregnant. And we named our baby Erik Gooden Jr.

I was so happy about getting married to Eric, but many weren't. I felt everyone was entitled to their own opinion of it. But that wouldn't stop us from becoming Mr. and Mrs. Gooden. We went to a small church called Pleasant Grove in Mossville, Mississippi, where Pastor Joe Keys united us in holy matrimony. I was no longer active in the church of my youth, but Eric and I did attend Pleasant Grove on occasion with his family. So that's where we chose to unite on February 12, 2010. It was one of the happiest days of my life, a day that I will never forget.

I remember the pastor telling us to speak our own vows to each other. Both of us were uncomfortable and nervous, but we spoke affectionately from our hearts. I remember what I said and what he said as if it happened yesterday. Officially, Mrs. Angela Gooden, I was floating on clouds. No one could ever know how deep the love that I had for this man went, it was unconditional, unbreakable.

After all the celebrating we began our chapter as "The Goodens." Finally no more relationship to relationship. I had a husband. That same year, I purchased my first mobile home and moved in across the street from my mom. My husband and I, our home together and that's where we would remain.

My husband and I lived, worked, loved, and partied together when we could. We were living our ideal happy life, "The Gooden's." A year after Erik Jr, I was pregnant with my fifth child, Aerica Gooden. My baby girl. She was named after my husband's twin sister. It was 2012 and we now had two girls and one boy together. We continued on living, loving, and cherishing each other daily. We worked and did what we needed to do to provide for our children.

I was a Certified Nurses Aide by this time. And it became my line of work for many years. I tried other occupations, but nothing satisfied me like nursing. I enjoyed taking care of the elderly and their needs. I learned a lot of things from some of them. Some felt like family to me. My husband was a poultry worker at a meat processing factory and a coil winder at a manufacturing plant.

We had ten years and counting together. That was the longest relationship I ever had; It was the longest he ever had. But just like any other relationship, our marriage became rocky. It started with the arguments here and there until they became constant. Arguments could be over a mistake, a misunderstanding, disrespect, over anything, and nothing at all.

Even though we argued we remained committed together. Things would go back to normal and then somewhere down the line, all hell would break loose again. Once again, another problem to solve, another misunderstanding, and the cycle would continue. Months would go by and we still stayed.

My marriage was real to me, we loved each other deeply, but we desperately needed someone to intervene. Our marriage was hurling out of control straight towards a cliff. Vows had been broken, I felt betrayed. On top of everything else, we were dealing with broken trust that led to more arguments, and then the abuse.

My children had grown up. They all could understand what was going on. We argued so much it disrupted my children's lives. They would run to my mom's house as soon as they'd hear us start up. They ran out of fear. I began living in fear. I put in a lot of tears and broke my back to try to keep it together, keep my family together, but I failed.

My children saw things I never intended for them to see. I had no one to talk to. I tried confiding in my family but that made it worse. Cops were called to our house so much, that they knew our street name Pnut & AO. That was an embarrassment to me and my children.

My husband had many issues, but he tried to be a great father to his children. However, the arguments went on, the abuse kept happening, and the children were still watching. In 2020, things really got crazy. I was at the point of giving up. I was tired of trying. Emotionally, mentally, and physically depleted, I had no more energy to give. I cried out to God for peace. I needed him in this marriage. I had wasted so much time trying to repair my marriage that I forgot about me, I forgot about my children.

I traveled off and on to Gulfport, Mississippi to catch little moments to breathe, to feel, and figure a way out. I was about to get my kids and leave, escape. But one fatal fight proved detrimental. My husband was abusing me something bad, and my oldest son didn't run this time. He tried to intervene, to protect me. In the chaos of it all, my son shot my husband. And Erik died that night.

People talked and said it was intentional but it wasn't. My son was a good kid. A basketball star, a great football player, and all year "A" and "B" honor roll student. Because of this tragedy, Joseph Jr trying to save me, he couldn't participate in his graduation ceremony. He still received his diploma with a 4.0 GPA, but he would not be able to continue his sports dreams of playing on a prestigious college team somewhere. All he had worked hard for, slipped out of his hands and no one could pick up the pieces.

There came the judgmental family members but where were they when I had bruises, black eyes, cried out for help? I felt they forgot about me; they knew the truth but didn't want to acknowledge it. I was trapped in a broken tunnel that I had no way of getting out of even during my failed attempts of trying. That was a real pain I had to deal with. I am still dealing with it. Many people watch victims of abuse from a safe distance, outside of the chaos, the whirlwind, and wonder, why do we stay? Why don't we get out? But that is just the thing...when you look at a tornado from outside of it, where you stand is calm and peaceful. But try being trapped in it, with winds and flying debris, and then tell me how easy it is to escape.

Reflection 4 - *What's Been Your Experience in Love*

What has been your experience falling in love? Are there certain relationships that have left a lasting effect on you (good, bad, the ugly)? How did you overcome a toxic relationship or are you still in it?

CHAPTER 5

The Road to Healing

ANXIETY AND DEPRESSION IS a sickness that can sometimes be unbearable to fight. Sometimes it makes you close yourself off from family, friends, and others. You don't want to be out in public, especially when you've suffered countless public pain, shame, and trauma. When I get overwhelmed with life itself that's when it bothers me the most. Sometimes I get nervous and my body starts to tremble. The smallest things make me flinch. I always say to myself, *if I can feel myself shake I know others notice too.* It's embarrassing but it's a part of me. I am still recovering, healing my way through this broken tunnel.

People can sometimes bring me down in the midst of it because they find it funny. I battle with it daily but I will not let it take over my life. I have been battling with it since a young girl, actually–anxiety and depression. As I look back, I can trace those times this thing in me got the best of me, had me all out of sorts, and making one bad decision after another. Unless you have it, no one understands how bad it feels to always worry, always be on edge, and suffer from something you don't quite understand. I must say with God's help, I'm winning. And I have had to come to the acceptance that *my wins* won't look like someone else's, and that's okay.

I was admitted into Pine Grove Mental Health Facility in Hattiesburg, MS. It's a place that I never thought I would have to go but it helped me in a desperate time of need. I met people who were battling with it just like I was. Some people were in worse condition than me. So before I go too deep down the "woe is me" hole, I know that it could have been worse. In Pine Grove, we had group meetings that allowed you to express yourself. In group meetings, I developed close relationships. It was nice having friends again. We talked, laughed, prayed, and sometimes cried together. In those moments, I knew that I wasn't alone.

Every day, we had to go to our room for an hour before we could come back out. In that hour, I would sit on my bed and pray, sing, and cry. Nurses would walk by and remark, "You have a beautiful voice." I'd look up, smile, and thank them.

No one truly knows my story or the things that I had to go through, even when they think they have me all figured out. No one could feel my pain or what it took to overcome the trenches at the bottom of this tunnel. My worship and my praise were for real!

At Pine Grove, nurses and doctors cared. I was put on different medicines until I found the right one that helped and made me feel normal as a person. One of my fears was getting something that didn't sync well with my body, because I have had a bad experience with medicines. Some make you feel normal, but some make your heart race, and some make you feel more panicky. At those times, I would always think of my children. I would motivate myself daily because I knew my children needed me. I fought for myself, I fought for them. I had to heal my way through this broken tunnel.

As a part of my recovery, I have been working to heal and cultivate healthier relationships. This is not easy, setbacks happen, but I am still in the game.

Friends: I never had luck with having many friends. I always got run over, and betrayed by them. I probably wasn't the best friend I could be either as I made mistakes and missteps along the way. Today my circle is very small. I choose wisely who I keep in my corner. Most of my friends are family. Alexis, that's my niece but my friend, my rider, and one of my supporters. When we're together we vent to each other and enjoy each other's company. She is one of my listening ears when no one else will listen. Alexis is funny, fun, and motivating. My niece, Deja is s friend as well. I call her sometimes to cry, to talk. We hang out and chill all the time. She is a great supporter too. She is one of the people who have seen my ups and downs. She is silly, sweet, smart, and very talented. Jasmine is another dear niece of mine. We don't get to hang out often but when we do, we always laugh. She's got a very funny way of laughing out loud that will make you laugh. She is laid back, outspoken, and hardworking but...sometimes a little lazy. It's never a dull moment when she is around! Keisha is a cousin and a friend. We've been hanging out since childhood. We have great conversations. She's always checking on me. She is hardworking, and amazing in many ways.

Today I remain friends with two ladies outside of my family: Kayla and Brandy. They are inspirational women. Kayla is like a sister to me. We look out for each other. When I was going through abuse, she was one of my biggest supporters. She would always fuss at me about knowing my worth. She would fuss with my husband about me. They couldn't get along at all. She was very outspoken and didn't care how you felt about it. This girl is so funny, she keeps me laughing and always joking, when I otherwise would just be crying. She should have been a bartender. She calls me over to have special drinks she makes and eat meals together. She makes great daiquiris and is a very good cook. Brandy is like a sister too. She has been one of my supporters. That's my dance partner! When we get together, it's hard getting us off the dance floor. We can't be stopped. Oh, and Ann is a friend I met over the years. When I was introduced to her family, I became family. She is a strong woman. Her talks made me stronger. I want all of them to know that they are appreciated for caring, loving me, and taking out time for me in my time of need. These girls have been a backbone that I could always depend on.

My Children: Over the years I have gained a relationship with all of my children. I am grateful for that. Angelica is the smart mouth one. She is hardworking and outspoken. People say we are just alike because she is the one I argue with. At times, we hang out and chill. I watch her and think, *my girl has grown up on me*. I am proud of the young lady that she has become. She graduated high school and has been working ever since. She is classy and unique. Family and friends call her Tweet, but I call her "My Little Jew" (my little jewel).

Joseph is smart, laid back, and always trying to be my daddy. It's always, "Ma, where you going, where you been, or where you going with that on!"

I always respond, "Boy, I'm grown and I'm the mama!"

He just sits back, looks at me, and grins. We have an amazing mother/son relationship. When we hang out, it's nothing but love and great vibes. I can always be myself around him. Family and friends call him Pole. I call him "My Pdawg".

Akeelah is a dancer like me. She is laid back. She struggles with friendships like I did and I worry for her. I always tell her, *"You'll always have a friend in your Mother."* She gets discouraged sometimes because she feels like everyone is against her. I encourage her to surround herself with positive people or stay to herself so she can be great in school and life.

When I dress up she's the one with all the compliments: "Mom, you look cute."

She is the one who takes my photos to post. She talks about me all the time on her Facebook page. That makes me feel like an awesome, loved mom. That's why in my sickness of anxiety and depression, while I might cry, slumber, go into a nervous attack, or completely fall apart, one thing is for sure, I will rise for myself and my children.

My children are the reason I fight every day. They are a reflection of me. My Erik Jr is a game player. He loves his PlayStation and iPad. The Roblox game is one of his favorites. If he is not at school, he's playing those games. Erik has a learning disability but he is very smart. He was my miracle baby. I had a high-risk pregnancy with him. I delivered him at eight months. The doctor told me that there could be a chance that his lungs wouldn't be developed at the time of birth. When he arrived in this world, he was okay. He loves sports, and he likes to eat! Erik is my jaw-kisser! I can be sitting on the couch minding my business and here he comes walking up and kissing me on the jaw. Sometimes he says, "*I love you, Mama.*" And I affectionately return the gesture. Those moments to me are priceless. Family and friends call him "Man" but I call him "My Lil Man."

Aerica is the baby of the bunch. She likes to eat too and play on the iPad. The Roblox game is one of her favorites as well. She is a momma's girl. Aerica is creative, silly, and careful who she makes friends with, but she's sweet. The family calls her "Fatmama." Friends call her Aerica. I call her Shawntae. I thank God for them all. These are my blessings.

My Marriage: My marriage has been so difficult to process through. I no longer have a husband to work through unresolved things with and say what I need to say. So I am left with all the scorched pieces to work through on my own. When I was dealing with problems in my marriage, I remember watching a movie called *War Room*. It was about this lady who was battling with things in her marriage. She was working and ran into this elderly lady. As they began to talk and got to know each other, the elderly lady told her to go into her secret closet where she could focus, write notes, and put them on the wall—everything that she needed God to do for her. Once she was done, she needed to pray. That movie inspired, motivated, uplifted me, and made me cry. So, I got into my secret closet, which was my bathroom. I began to make notes and attached them to my wall. After that, I began to pray. That's when things begin to shift. I would always write something about my husband and me. I would also write concerns for my children. One thing that I didn't do was put down what I needed to change. I started learning about God and the amazing things that he could do. It was all new to me but for my life, my children, and my marriage, I was willing to try. Never would I have seen coming what happened, how it all ended. Now I am somewhere in the thick of it, trying to figure out where God's plan is in it all. I have faith, it is somewhere in the ugliness of it all, and one day I will see it clearly and come to acceptance of it.

Out of my husband's family, I could only get along with two people: his sisters. His twin passed away. His other sister still shows me respect as his wife. It bothered me not to connect with my mother-in-law. But we always bumped heads somewhere down the line. I still loved her despite that. God is love and so am I. So, maybe God will continue to heal in all these areas as well.

My Relationship with Me: This tunnel I am navigating through is filled with damaged puzzle pieces but healed mended parts as well. I have ugly truths but major comebacks. In this tunnel of life, I have had many disappointments, setbacks, breakdowns, embarrassments, rumors, hatred, threats, being mistreated, mistreating myself, and much more. I learned that the best lesson you could ever learn was a taught one. I keep learning more, I keep growing more. I am working each day to love myself better, and loving myself better means more than just saying the word but doing things to help me not hurt me. I could never go back in life and change the beginning or the in-betweens but I do have control over my now. One of the hardest things that I had to do was let go of betrayal, feeling guilty, and anger. I am grateful for my past. Painful, yes, but some things I will never regret. I can't live in the regrets if I am to move forward.

Reflection 5 - *Your Mental Health*

How are you working on strengthening your mental health? Have you assessed where you are now, why you do the things you do, and what steps you can take to become a better version of yourself (for you first, then for your loved ones)?

CHAPTER 6

Joy Comes in the Morning

I KNOW THAT YOU have to hurt to know. You have to fall in life to grow. You have to lose to win. Some of life's most valuable lessons are taught through pain. One of the hardest life lessons is letting go. Letting go of loss. Letting go of guilt. Letting go of feeling betrayed. Letting go of old friends, letting go of some family. I have fought to hold on and I have fought to let go *while healing in this broken tunnel.*

Through it all, I told myself to stay strong because one day I knew I was gonna be able to look back and say, "Through the storm, through the rain, in this broken tunnel, through the pain, I made it."

Weeping may endure for a night, but joy comes in the morning...I couldn't heal because I kept pretending to people, to myself that I wasn't hurt *while stumbling in this broken tunnel.*

Looking back over my life, I thought winning meant keeping everything together when everyone else expects you to fall apart. It's so annoying how people who know nothing about you have the most to say. If someone hasn't been in my shoes then surely they can't tell me how to lace them up. But I'm learning to stop trying to prove, *I'm good and I got it together,* to people. What is the point of trying to prove others wrong, but falling apart all the same behind closed doors?

Truth is, I am weak, I've been broken, and now suffer from anxiety and depression. Admitting my weakness is the strongest thing I could do for myself. There is a Bible passage that explains, In my weakness, I am made strong because then I am willing to lean on God's strength. Surrender myself to his will, and stop trying to fix everything by myself.

Growth is a never-ending process for me. I am still learning as I grow. I have failed in many things in my life. I have also had many distractions. I made mistakes and forgot who I was. But, I got back up and *I am healing in a broken tunnel*!

In life, it seems as if the most loyal people are the ones that are treated the worse. It's something I am processing through. But in the end, we win, I tell myself. At this point in my tunnel, I've decided that I do not need anyone distracting my peace because they can't find their own or don't want to live in peace. Misery loves company and I am tired of keeping that type of fellowship. I have noticed, my mindset is changing. My priorities have changed. In this tunnel, I have learned to motivate myself. I tell myself, ***no matter what happens in life you are not your situation and it does not define you***, *while healing in this broken tunnel*.

In this tunnel, there were times I had no one to turn to but God. That was my strength. That was when I told myself ***when you have no one else to stand for you, stand for yourself***. I am not fully healed from my past, but I am moving forward because I owe it to myself, and my children to be happy again *while healing in this broken tunnel*.

I am going to be better than what broke me. I'm turning my shame into grace. I am growing in this tunnel from the dirt that people threw on my name. I am humbled enough to know that I am not better than anyone but I am wise enough to know that I am different and better than who they say I am. Pain shaped me into disfigurement. Pain made me into something bitter. ***I want to be made over.***

In the darkness of this tunnel, I felt trapped, there was no way out.

In the tunnel, sticks and stones were thrown.

In the tunnel, people laughed at my pain.

In the tunnel, fear plagued me.

In the tunnel, I was disrespected as a wife.

In the tunnel, I lost family and friends.

In the tunnel, I lost my children.

In the tunnel, I lost love.

In the tunnel, I lost me.

Some of you today may be trapped in a broken tunnel. Some may feel that there's no way out. Some of you may want to leave the tunnel but fail to leave because you are living in fear. Many of you may be on your way out and wondering "*Is there life after a broken tunnel?*"

I say, "Yes!" to you today. There is life after a broken tunnel. I was the tunnel, bruised and broken. I am now working my way out of ***me***. We can be our ***own*** worst enemy.

In the light, I am healing, working my way out of this broken tunnel.

Today, as I work through this tunnel, I've gained two grand boys who I truly adore. In this tunnel, I took my life lesson and sprouted new roots. In this tunnel, I threw aside fear and became brave. When I became brave, I gained courage. In this tunnel, I was reunited with my children. In this tunnel, I used the sticks and stones and built a village! In this tunnel, I am being made strong. In this tunnel, I have light. In this tunnel, I am feeling peace where there once was only chaos. I feel the warmth of the sun on my skin, *Mama*, and I am being made whole.

In this tunnel, I have Joy.

In this tunnel, I have a reason to smile.

In this tunnel, I found the love of God.

In this tunnel, I found Me.

In this tunnel, you now know my story, but only I know my pain. In this tunnel, you will never fully grasp the steps I had to take to get to where I am today. In this tunnel, I took everything that was meant to break me and made something beautiful. In this tunnel, I am now living. In this tunnel, I might bend, crack, or stumble but I won't be destroyed.

In this tunnel, I have a praise!

In this tunnel, the chains are being broken and are falling. I am a woman becoming loosed. I'm being made whole. That chain was me, weighted down and bound. I am now working my way out of **me**. We can be our **own** worst enemy.

The glory of life is intertwined with the falling and rising. And rising looks like whatever it needs to look like for you. But, "*Rise up, my sister. Rise up!*"

I wrote this *Healing in a Broken Tunnel* reflective story as part of my healing and recovery. But I also wrote it for you. To build up women like me, a broken tunnel, torn down and crumbled, but not destroyed. Your tunnel may be cloudy, dark, or foggy, but the sun, *Mama*, will shine again. You are not utterly destroyed. *You will survive and heal through a broken tunnel.*

HEALING IN A BROKEN TUNNEL

Words of Encouragement

Words of Encouragement to All of the Women Living, Losing, and Loving In A Broken Tunnel

1. Live a life of purpose

2. Use your time wisely

3. You cannot truly love another until you love yourself

4. Love your children

5. Believe in yourself

6. Be grateful

7. Positivity always wins

8. Pray

9. Do good and good will come to you

10. Life is beautiful and so are you!

Contact the Author

ALL THANKS TO GOD! BATTLES COULDN'T
BREAK ME, ENEMIES COULDN'T SHAKE ME.
TEARS KEPT FLOWING BUT I KEPT GOING.
WHO DID IT...GOD DID IT FOR ME!

If you would like to send a special message to the author or contact for interviews, email:

authorangelagooden@gmail.com

Made in the USA
Columbia, SC
07 April 2024

33913041R00029